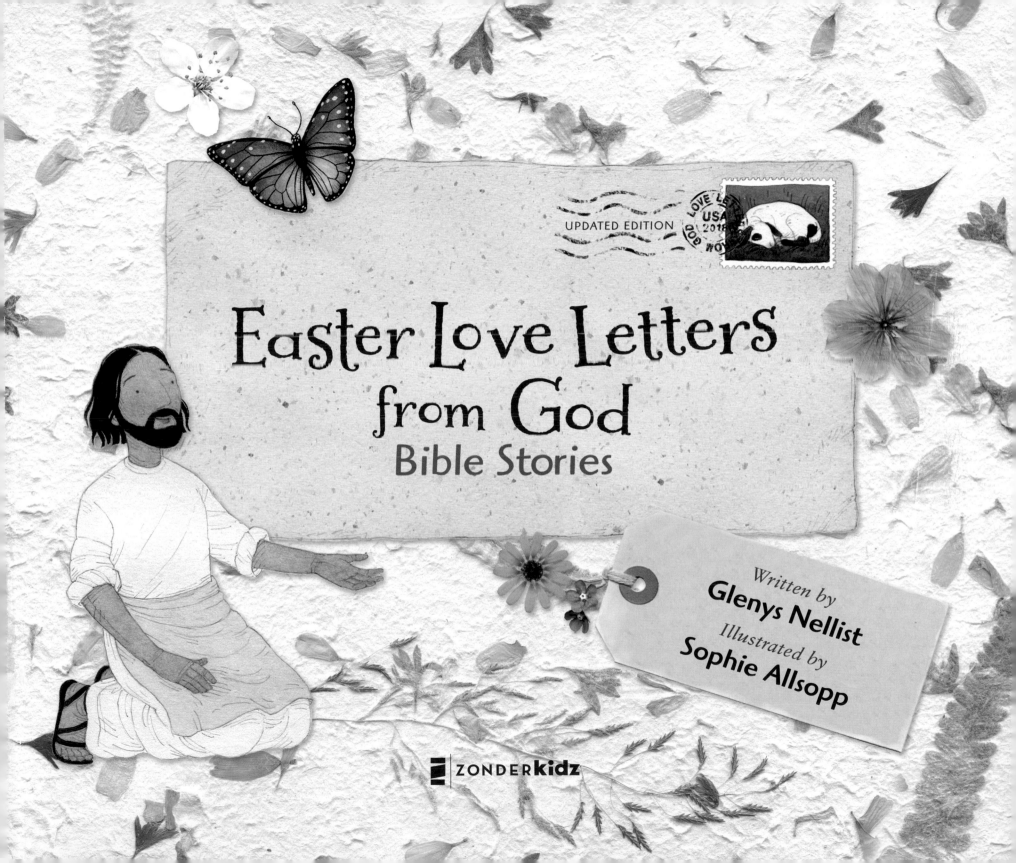

UPDATED EDITION

LOVE LETTERS USA 2018 GOD

Easter Love Letters
from God
Bible Stories

Written by
Glenys Nellist

Illustrated by
Sophie Allsopp

ZONDER**kidz**

This book is dedicated to the one
who made me the Secret Suppers.
I do miss you.
—G.N.

For Wendy, in memory of Peter.
With love,
S.A.

ZONDERKIDZ

Easter Love Letters from God, Updated Edition
Copyright © 2018 by Glenys Nellist
Illustrations © 2018 by Sophie Allsopp

This title is also available as a Zondervan ebook.

Requests for information should be addressed to:

Zonderkidz, 3900 Sparks Dr. SE, Grand Rapids, Michigan 49546

ISBN 978-0-310-15477-8

Art direction and design: Jody Langley

Printed in India

23 24 25 26 27 28 /REP/ 22 21 20 19 18 17 16 15 14 13 12 11 10 9 8 7 6 5 4 3 2 1

Contents

King of Kings....................4
Ride Into Jerusalem

What Love Looks Like..............8
Washing Feet

The Secret Supper...................12
Last Supper

The Gloomy Garden................16
Gethsemane

The Darkest Day..................20
Crucifixion

The Quiet Cave...................24
Burial

The Super Surprise 28
Resurrection

King of Kings

Matthew 21:1–11

The donkey felt very special as he trotted down the road into Jerusalem with Jesus on his back. He had never carried a king before! The road was lined with people clapping and cheering. Everyone was there to welcome Jesus. Little children laughed as they waved their palm branches high in the air like flags. "Hosanna! Hosanna!" the crowd shouted, as Jesus passed by. He was the one they had heard about. Here was the king who could save them from their enemies. But how would he do that? He wasn't wearing armor, and he didn't look like he was ready for a fight. An earthly king would ride on a mighty horse. But Jesus was a heavenly king. He rode in on a quiet donkey. An earthly king would ride in with an army of strong soldiers. But Jesus rode in with an army of invisible angels. An earthly king would ride in carrying gleaming swords and weapons. But Jesus rode in carrying love, forgiveness, and peace. An earthly king would capture his enemies and take them to jail. But Jesus would free his enemies with love and lead them to heaven.

The King of Kings stepped down from his donkey, patted it on the back, and turned toward Jerusalem. Jesus had only a few days left to live on earth—just a few days to show the world what love looked like. And so, his last days began …

God's Wonderful Words to You

I am the LORD who heals you.
Exodus 15:26

Dear _____,

When Jesus rode into Jerusalem, he didn't come to fight the Romans. My son came to fight hatred, sadness, and unkindness. And the only way to fight those enemies is with love. Jesus came to teach people how to love. He came to heal us from everything that hurts us, and to fill our lives with joy, hope, forgiveness, and peace. The more you get to know Jesus, the more you'll discover that this can be your life too.

Love,

GOD

What Love Looks Like

John 13:1–17

The disciples were excited. Jesus had invited them to a secret supper. But they'd been walking through the dusty streets of Jerusalem all day. By the time they reached the special room, their feet would be filthy! Thank goodness a servant would be there to wash their feet for them. They didn't want to have dirty feet at dinnertime. They were going to eat with a King!

But a surprise was waiting for the disciples.
When they arrived at the room, there was no
servant there. Jesus was kneeling on the floor.
A bowl of soapy water was next to him. And
he had a towel tied around his waist.

9

Right there, in that room, Jesus showed his disciples what love looked like. He took their feet in his hands, and washed them, just like a servant would. The hands that created the world washed their feet. The special one from heaven made the disciples feel like *they* were the special ones.

10

"That is what love looks like," Jesus said. "Love tells people how special they are. Love makes someone feel wonderful. When I am gone, go into the world and take love with you."

The disciples didn't understand that Jesus was going to leave them. But they understood what love looked like—because the King of Love had shown them.

God's Wonderful Words to You
If you love one another, everyone will know you are my disciples.
John 13:35

Dear _____,

Did you know that the disciples did what Jesus asked them? They never forgot how Jesus washed their feet that night. They never forgot how much Jesus loved them. So they took that love into the world. And you can do the same. Never forget how much Jesus loves you. Show that love to others. If you do that, everyone will know you are one of his disciples.

Love,

GOD

11

The Secret Supper

Luke 22:14–20 & John 14:1–6

The disciples were ready for their secret supper with Jesus. Their feet were clean. The table was set. They were hungry. But Jesus was quiet. His eyes were sad as he looked around the table at his friends. He knew this was the last meal he would ever eat with them. Jesus picked up a loaf of bread and broke it. The disciples watched as crumbs fell to the table.

"This broken bread is like my body," Jesus said. "My body will be broken for you."

Then Jesus took a pitcher of wine. The disciples watched in the quiet as he filled the cup. "Whenever you eat bread, and whenever you drink wine, remember me."

What did Jesus mean? The disciples were scared. It sounded like he was going to leave them.

13

God's Wonderful Words to You

I am the way.
John 14:6

"Don't let your hearts be troubled," Jesus said. "I'm going somewhere wonderful. You can't come with me yet. But one day, I will come back and take you there. It's a beautiful, happy place, with lots of rooms. It's a home that's big enough for everyone, and I'm going to get it ready for you."

The disciples were still worried. How would they know how to get to the special place? But Jesus told them. "I am the way," Jesus whispered. "Believe in me. Be like me. Live like me. Love like me. Because I am the way to heaven."

Dear _____,

Close your eyes. I want you to imagine a big, beautiful home with so many rooms you can't count them. Imagine every room is filled with love, laughter, and happiness. It's a place you never want to leave, because of all the fun, joy, and peace there. Open your eyes. You just imagined my home in heaven! Jesus wants everyone in the whole world to live there with him. And the best part is that my home is not hard to find. All you need to do is believe in Jesus, and he will show you the way.

Love,
GOD

The Gloomy Garden

Mark 14:32–42

Darkness fell as the disciples followed Jesus out into the night. Jesus walked through the quiet streets toward the Garden of Gethsemane. He wanted to pray. The moon shined through the olive trees as Jesus knelt down. The garden was gloomy. All was still.

"God, are you there?"

There was no reply.

Jesus sobbed. He didn't want to die. But he trusted God. And even though he felt all alone, he knew that God was with him. He was ready.

The sound of heavy footsteps broke the silence of the night. Angry shouts filled the air. Jesus looked up through his tears. Shadowy figures came toward him, torches flickering in the darkness. The soldiers were there to take him away. Jesus stood up. It was time to go.

God's Wonderful Words to You

I am always with you.
Matthew 28:20

Dear _____,

Have you ever felt alone, like Jesus did that night? When you feel like that, I want you to remember something very important. You are never alone. I am always by your side. Those soldiers might have taken Jesus away from the garden, but they could never take him away from me. And there is nothing that can ever take you away from me either. Remember this promise ... I am always with you.

Love,

GOD

19

The Darkest Day

Matthew 27:45–54

High on the hillside, Jesus hung on the cross. Jesus was ready to die, but he was still afraid.

He could not breathe. He felt all alone. Where was God now?

The sun disappeared behind a huge gray cloud. Cold crept in. Darkness covered the world. Jesus closed his eyes. He bowed his head. He took one last breath. And at three o'clock in the afternoon, in that cold and darkness, Jesus died.

The wind howled. The whole earth trembled. The rocks shattered. The hills quaked. And the mighty curtain in the temple split in two. But Jesus was still.

It was finished.

Dear _____,

Shall I tell you a secret? When Jesus was crying on the cross, I was crying too. When Jesus felt all alone, I felt all alone too. And when my son died, part of me died too. But guess what? Death does not win in this story! Life wins! Love wins! My promise to Jesus was that nothing could separate him from my love. And that is the same promise I give to you.

Love,

GOD

God's Wonderful Words to You

Nothing at all can ever separate us from God's love.

Romans 8:39

The Quiet Cave

John 19:38–42

Jesus had died. Joseph and Nicodemus were sad. They carefully took Jesus' body down from the cross. They cleaned him. They wrapped his body in strips of white linen and carried him to a quiet cave on the hillside. They laid Jesus down inside the cave. Then they said goodbye. Before they left, they rolled a big stone over the entrance.

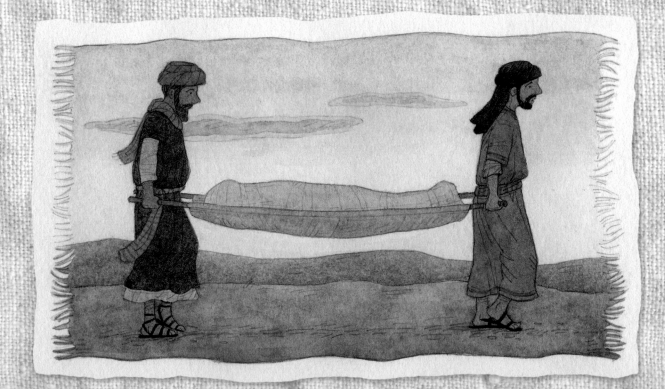

Outside the cave, two guards kept watch.
The big heavy stone was sealed in place. And
for three whole days, all was still.

Dear _____,

Do you like surprises? Inside that quiet cave, I was working on a surprise that no one could imagine. It would be the greatest surprise the world had ever known. Something was happening to Jesus. My son was going to have a brand-new life. But for three whole days, the world had to wait.

Love,

GOD

But *inside* that quiet cave God was working. If you tried to peek inside, you couldn't see anything. If you stood outside and put your ear to the big stone, you couldn't hear anything. If you tried to imagine what was happening, you couldn't. But inside, God was doing something utterly amazing. Something only God could do. Jesus waited. And the world held its breath and waited with him.

God's Wonderful Words to You

I am about to do something new.
Isaiah 43:19

27

The Super Surprise

Mark 16:1–7

There was something special about the day. The birds that lived in the trees above the quiet cave knew it. They knew it when they opened their eyes that morning and saw the sunrise. The sun peeked out over the horizon and seemed to wink at the world. Pinks and oranges, yellows and reds flooded the sky. Golden rays reached out like fingers toward the cave and twinkled as if they were holding a secret.

The birds could feel an early morning whisper, a song, gliding through the trees. And now, the birds could *hear* it—a whisper that got louder as it danced along. It was a name. A name carried on the wind, sailing through the leaves, rushing through the grass. The birds perked up and opened their beaks to join the chorus of all creation as every living thing sang the name, the name that is above any other name.

"Jesus! Jesus! Jesus is alive!"

jesus is alive!

29

The big stone had been moved. The cave was empty. The sun was shining. Jesus, King of the whole world, was alive again! The trees clapped their hands. The flowers danced for joy. The birds flew high over the fields and carried the news—the most wonderful news that the world has ever heard—Jesus is alive!

And soon, Mary Magdalene would know it, the disciples would know it, Jesus's mother would know it. One day, everyone in the whole world would know it. And now, you know it too.

Dear _____,

Can you believe that my son, Jesus, came back to life? Only the King of the whole world could do that. Jesus is the King of Love, the King of Hope, and the King of Heaven. And he wants to be the King of your life too. Will you let him? I hope you do!

I Love You,
GOD

God's Wonderful Words to You

You are all children of God by believing in Christ.
Galatians 3:26

Thank you, God, for Jesus,
And how he loves me so.
Here's my little letter—
There's something you should know.

Even though I'm only young,
I know your love is true.
I hope you'll read my words and see
I really love you too.

Dear GOD,

_____

_____

_____

_____

_____

_____

Love,

_____